The Holy Spirit in a Heart of Grace

Grace Wallis

Scripture quotations are taken from
KJV Bible and Living Bible

Cover image and dove illustration used
under license from Shutterstock.com

Book design by Mark Morgan

ISBN-13: 978-1539810384
ISBN-10: 1539810380

CONTENTS

PREFACE

Writing Grace's story was a privilege and a blessing. We became friends through our Ladies Sunday School class. She shared with me that God had told her to write a book of her journey with the Holy Spirit, but had no idea how to put it into words. The desire to do what God had told her, however, burned in her heart. She felt God had brought us together for that purpose. After praying and considering her request, I agreed. Months and months of meeting together, talking, sharing, shedding tears at times, and praying followed. Her excitement at relating how the Holy Spirit had worked in her life was a spiritual blessing to me personally.

My hope is that I have captured her feelings in a way that conveys her love, devotion and faith to our Heavenly Father who truly is the center of every facet of her life. Grace's hope is that her story inspires every reader to seek that same wonderful, daily relationship with Him.

Sunny Stiner

Acknowledgments

Thinking back over the years of my journey, there are so many people who come to mind that I want to thank for encouraging me in various ways. The first person I think of is my former pastor, Sam Matthews. Each time I went to him and voiced my conviction that God was calling me to go to a particular country, his answer was always the same: we will pray about it. And I knew in my heart he and his wife, Kathy, would follow through on that promise. Just knowing they were holding me up in prayer throughout my ministry sustained me through so many difficult times. But it wasn't just Brother Sam's prayers that helped. Every time I felt called to a country, I would tell him and he always knew someone there I could either stay with or call to arrange a place. It never ceased to amaze me that he had friends or connections in so many faraway places. I will always remember him and his gracious wife for showing me, in so many ways, their love for God and for me with their support and prayers.

Another wonderful couple I met along the way was Major Dave Helseth and his wife, Lucie. They took me in to their home while I was in Nairobi and welcomed me as a part of their family. I cannot thank them enough for being my very good friends, and also allowing me to live completely rent free for over four years in a home they owned in my hometown. My heart will be forever grateful.

This book would not have been possible had it not been for Sunny Stiner who took my experiences and my journey and found the words to express my heartfelt feelings. Before I met her, I was reading my Bible one day and God spoke to me, saying, "Write a book." After much prayer, I began to think about all the things He had brought me to and through. I knew I could not begin to put into words all He had done for me throughout my lifetime. Knowing I wanted to obey God, but realizing my inability to express myself, I said to the Father, "You sent Aaron to speak for Moses; send someone to help me write this book." He sent Sunny. After long talks and shared prayer, it was apparent she had the God-given talent needed to put my journey into words.

Through the following months, as I related my story to her, she shared with me that she knew God had given her a gift of insight into my feelings, my reactions and my love for Jesus. Her ability to express my thoughts, fears, joy and devotion to my Lord was brought about only by the anointing of the Holy Spirit working through both our lives. Thanks be to God for giving me an "Aaron" to speak for me and someone who could write the words contained in this book as though I had spoken them myself.

And finally, to all the ones known and unknown, who have offered up prayers on my behalf and provided encouragement to me in so many ways through the years, thank you from the bottom of my heart.

Grace Wallis

CHAPTER 1

Saving Grace

You could say my journey began on January 9, 1925, the date of my first birth. Little did I know at that time Jehovah God, my creator, had fashioned and knit me in my mother's womb, knew me by name and loved me with an everlasting love even before I was born. When I look back now and recall how names had a meaning in Biblical times, I cannot think of any name that would describe my journey and my lifelong walk with God more than the name given to me—Grace. I like to think God put that name in my mother's heart, knowing my future would require, and thus be given, so much of His grace.

I grew up on a farm with three brothers and one sister where I learned to milk cows, pick cotton and do any other chores necessary on a farm which I was old enough to perform. My father always saw that we attended church regularly. He was both a deacon and the church song leader and my mother was a Sunday school teacher. I have many fond memories as a very young child standing beside my father as he led the hymns. The beautiful words to those hymns and the powerful Word of God were a very important part of my life as I grew up. Both reached deep into my heart and I realized more and more at a young age that Jesus loved *even me*, little Grace Akins.

Since our family attended church on a regular basis, I went forward many times through the years to be saved. I realize now the reason. No one had ever fully explained God's plan of salvation, nor was I ever told about the sinner's prayer and what the words really meant. Up until that time, a void had remained in my heart and peace was not my constant companion. It wasn't until the age of sixteen that I fully understood the sinner's prayer and what Christ's birth, life, death and resurrection meant to me. From the moment I genuinely prayed that meaningful prayer and accepted Christ into my heart—which I now refer to as my second birth—I felt the love of God flood my soul and become real to me for the first time. The empty void was forever gone. A change had taken place and a feeling of peace and overwhelming love filled my heart.

Whenever alone, or with friends or family, I felt the contentment that comes only after one has accepted the grace found through the salvation of an all-loving, eternal God. As far back as I can remember, I always felt Jesus was with me. But after my salvation experience, I was unmistakably a new creature in Christ and *all* things became new. From that day forward, that love has affected every aspect of my life.

What a wonderful gift and blessing it was to be raised in a Godly home and to have been exposed to the wonder of God's grace and love. When I see and hear of so many sad and tragic circumstances of children being raised in an atmosphere of ungodliness, drugs, and neglect, my heart aches for them. My spirit prays for them. "There but for the grace of God go I." I have to pause in thankfulness, even now, and say "Praise God from whom all blessings flow. Thank you, Heavenly Father, for a Godly father and mother."

After my salvation experience, I was ever aware of God's constant presence. Being as young as I was, I still knew without a doubt that I had a friend like no other—one who walked beside me each day, caring for me in a way no earthly person could. Even the love my parents expressed for me had never filled my heart in the way Christ's love did. It was a wonderful new awakening of His nearness and presence. No longer did God seem far away or like a storybook hero, but real and alive and *always* beside me. Knowing this, I felt it only natural that, in any situation, I talked to God as I would a special friend. It was not unusual at all for me to tell Him about my fears, my anxieties, and yes, my problems. Always, I was looking to Him for answers and experiencing the peace only He could give in knowing I could trust Him for the divine guidance I needed.

After accepting Christ, there were incidents when I would just start weeping in church without knowing why. My mother would question me after returning home and would ask what was wrong. I could never answer her as I did not know myself what was taking place. It was not until later in life I came to understand I had been chosen by God to be an intercessor and it was the Holy Spirit within me, grieving and weeping over the lost. Those same feelings remain to this day.

The next two years or so were basically uneventful as to any monumental things happening in my life. I continued to experience the constant presence of God, and through prayer and the reading of His word, began to know Him in a deeper way.

I graduated from high school in 1943 at the age of eighteen. Two of my brothers were in the military at the time; my older brother being in the army and the younger being in the navy. Like so many young impressionable people, I felt since they were both serving their country, I should do the same. So I joined the army. After joining, I decided if I was going to be a military person, I should look like one. I cut off my long hair and got rid of all my "girly" clothes in an effort to present a more serious soldier image.

A few days after being sworn in, but before receiving my orders, a phone call came saying they were no longer taking women in the military. Needless to say, I was very disappointed—especially since I had already gone to so much effort to look the part. It was some time and some expense later before I shed my soldier image and regained my natural feminine look. So much for my "stars and stripes" appearance. A short time later, I received my discharge papers which I proudly preserve to this day. It's still a good feeling to know that I tried to perform my patriotic duty.

My, how things have changed. Now we have females performing nearly all the duties which men perform, including being fighter pilots. I suppose if God's chosen people, the Israelites, have decided their women can serve in all capacities to defend the land God gave them, we can only hope that God approves of our country doing the same.

After the disappointing news that I could not join the military, I remained at home and began attending Draughon's Business School to become a secretary. It was a career many young girls chose at that time. I had no means of transportation and had to walk everywhere, including back and forth to attend business school. After doing this for a while, I decided to rent a sleeping room closer to the school and eliminate at least some of the walking.

While attending school, God continued to watch over me and I was offered a job at a loan company, ending my short attendance in business school. While working for the loan company, I was asked if I would teach a 4th grade class in a nearby town as all the teachers had gone to work at the shipyards in California due to the war effort. I accepted the teaching position and rode the train back and forth many days as I still had no means of transportation. Many times, I would stay with one of the local families at night so I could be there the next morning for work.

After only one semester of teaching, I was called and asked if I would like to work for the Oklahoma Legislature as a typist in a stenographic pool while they were in session. I regretted in some ways having to leave the children at the school, but could not pass up the financial opportunity. God continued to provide one job after another, and each time, the opportunities and changes were always to my benefit. It was amazing to see how God took care of me during this period. His watch-care served to strengthen my faith and I relied on Him more and more, realizing that He was a God I could trust in *all* things. My love *for* Him and my trust *in* Him continued to grow stronger through the realization He was always mindful of my every need.

> "GOD WILL MEET ALL YOUR NEEDS ACCORDING
> TO HIS GLORIOUS RICHES IN CHRIST JESUS."
> (PHILIPPIANS 4:19)

I attended a church in Shawnee and eventually met and married a young man. My 20-year marriage could only be described as unhappy. My husband was a dominating, controlling person. It was an emotional daily struggle to cope with his changing moods and erratic behavior. Every night, I would kneel by my boys' beds and pray, asking God to watch over and protect them. I knew God's hand was on them and that assurance alone helped me get through each difficult day of emotional upheaval. Looking back, I realize it was by God's grace I was able to endure the verbal abuse and stress.

CHAPTER 2

Hearing God's Voice

The first time God spoke audibly to me was when my oldest son, Bob, had graduated from high school. My heart's desire was that he could go to college. However, we did not have the necessary finances. God knew the desires I envisioned for my son and how I longed to see it come to pass. One Wednesday night as I sat in church waiting to give the monthly report, I heard a voice say to me, "Your son Bobby Jack will go to college." I turned to see who had spoken. No one was near me. I knew at once it was God who had spoken. You can imagine the awesome feeling I had, knowing the God whom I worshiped, loved and trusted had actually given me the privilege of hearing His voice.

As soon as church was over, I rushed home to tell my husband and sons God had spoken to me, personally, and told me Bobby Jack was going to college. Naturally, their first question was "Where?" I replied I didn't know because I was so overwhelmed at hearing God's voice I had forgotten to ask. However, I assured them I knew without a doubt Bob was going because God had spoken.

This was in July. It seemed every door was shut and nothing was happening that pointed toward Bob being able to go to college. Then my brother called one evening and said he had heard Oral Roberts was opening a new university in Tulsa, Oklahoma, and suggested Bobby call and see if he could try out for a basketball scholarship. We called. Bobby did try out, received the scholarship and graduated in 1969. My dream of seeing both my boys getting a college education was fulfilled when my youngest son, Jerry, received a two-year scholarship from a college in our hometown. After graduating, he received another two-year scholarship from St. Edwards in Austin, completing his college education. Once more, God's promise of provision was fulfilled. And once more, I recognized and acknowledged the mercy and care God provides for his children.

"FOR THE LORD IS GOOD. HIS UNFAILING LOVE CONTINUES FOREVER AND HIS FAITHFULNESS CONTINUES TO EACH GENERATION." (PSALM 100:5)

My faith was growing stronger with each manifestation of the ever-present God being directly involved in my life. Even more amazing to me was the fact God had spoken to me, Grace Wallis, and this realization just increased my fervent desire to know more and more of Him.

My marriage, however, continued to be a very unhappy one. After years of tension and struggling, I still remember God speaking plainly to my heart, saying, "That's enough… you don't have to take this anymore." I then knew what

I had to do, and more importantly, that what I had to do was with God's blessing. My younger son was still at home, and previous to this time, my husband had continually threatened to take my son away from me if I divorced him. Somehow, he convinced me that he could. But knowing I was God's child and He did not want me to suffer any longer, I had the courage to ask him for a divorce.

Not wanting to put my son through the turmoil I felt would follow, I told my husband I would consent to him having custody. Saying those words broke my heart, even knowing I had God's blessing in my decision. But to my amazement and indescribable relief, he said he did not want custody and would agree to the divorce. He moved out that night. Once again, as through the years, God stood in the gap for me. His hand in removing me from that situation and leaving my beloved son with me proved, as the song says, "Christ is Enough For Me." My belief that with God, all things are possible, was reinforced even more.

I had gone to work for the Sonic Corporation's attorney at a good salary prior to my husband leaving. After he moved out, I was left with a vehicle which was not paid for and living in a house with a mortgage payment. I became responsible for these two payments with very little financial assistance from my ex-husband. Each day, my concerns grew as I wondered how I would make these payments. But again, as in the past, the telephone rang one day with a job offer at the Oklahoma Highway Department. The best news was I could continue to keep books for Sonic, thus having the benefit of two incomes rather than one. Through God's grace and provision, my load was lightened, and a way was provided for me. The promises of God are limitless and He keeps them *always*. I can truthfully say I have a friend in high places who makes things happen.

I continued attending my church, but many people there were of the opinion that God does not speak to people today as He once did. That opinion is shared by many today. But I stood even stronger in my faith, knowing without a doubt God had spoken to me. I have never read anywhere in scripture that He has quit speaking to His people. Until I do, I will continue to listen to His voice and follow where He leads.

A few years later as I sat with the treasurer to pay the monthly church bills, God gave me a vision of a new church. I shared my vision with the church one Wednesday night, and a vote was taken to see about the possibility of a new building. I was appointed head of the building committee. Throughout this time, I was attending all the meetings I could at Oral Roberts University, still desiring the outpouring of the Holy Spirit.

In the meantime, the new church building was becoming a reality, slowly but surely, according to God's timing. We applied for a loan from The Baptist Foundation of Oklahoma and still lacked $2,000 to finish the ceiling. After a meeting with the building committee and praying that this need be met, two people—one of whom did not even attend our church—made donations of $1,000 each. I know God's angels, in so many ways, had spread the word of our financial need and laid it on the hearts of these two people to give.

CHAPTER 3

Accepting God's Gift

On the Sunday the new building was to be dedicated, I was driving and passed a building when the Lord spoke to me, saying, "Turn in here." Since it was the Sunday I was to give my tithe to my home church, I said, "Next time I will." I had no idea what was in the building. Sometime later, I did go back to the place and a new church was just starting up. I went in and stayed for the entire service. When the pastor concluded his message, he said that anyone who desired the infilling of the Holy Spirit with evidence of speaking in tongues should come forward. I went forward, and as I did, I received what I had been praying and longing for…the infilling of the Holy Spirit.

Words cannot describe the complete joy and wonderful peace that encompassed my soul. It would be like trying to tell someone who doesn't know God what a personal relationship with Him is like; it is impossible until you experience it yourself. Since the moment I opened my heart to the fullness of the Holy Spirit, my life and reason for living have never been the same. That experience only

11

increased my desire to know God more deeply. I prayed more. I read my Bible more. I knew Jesus loved me and I kept professing my love for Him. But telling Him with my mouth was nothing compared to the joy I felt when my love for Him went from my mouth to the depths of my heart. That was the day I *really* fell in love with Jesus. The more time I spent with Him, the more I loved Him. I would go to church and spend the entire night in prayer and worship, just talking to Him as I would my dearest friend. I poured out my love, concerns and needs, seeking answers and guidance from the one who knows all things. The Bible became my closest companion and God revealed more and more of Himself as I absorbed all the beautiful words breathed by God himself.

It was prophesied over me by my pastor, Brother Sam, that I had been called by God to be an intercessor. What a blessed privilege to pray on behalf of others. The more I prayed, the more He directed my footsteps. When I walked, the spirit of prayer was upon me and the Holy Spirit prayed through me as I spoke in tongues. I delighted in knowing that I was, indeed, a servant of the Holy God and being used for his purposes. I was happiest when praying, and God never disappointed me as my faith grew.

One Sunday, as I was on my way to church, I heard the Father say, "You will take my Word around the world." I didn't know what to think or answer at the time. I pondered it for several days in my heart and then heard God say, "I have spoken." I knew then one day I would go as God had directed, having no idea what was ahead of me.

In the fall of 1983, my church went on a weekend retreat. I had never been to one before and was very excited, but didn't know what to expect. At the retreat, the pastor told us to each go somewhere and get alone with God. When we came back together, I sat in the very back seat. As we sang, God spoke to me and said, "Dance before me." I just sat there somewhat hesitant. Again, He spoke to me and said, "Dance before me." I answered, "I don't know how." "Stand up," He said, so I stood up and then heard "Turn around." As I turned, He spoke again, "Turn around and turn again." I began to spin in a circle and it was like my feet never touched the ground. It was such a wonderful and freeing feeling. As I sat down, God said, "Dance before my people." All this was so new to me, but I wanted to follow as God directed.

The next Sunday morning in the worship service, God spoke again, saying, "Dance before me." I obeyed and danced as I did at the retreat. In looking back, I feel sure it was the first time anyone had ever danced in our church. But through my open willingness to obey God's direction, the people of God in the church were also freed to dance before the Lord. I still marvel at how this freedom of worship blessed our church.

I realize it is not acceptable in so many churches today to raise our hands in praise and worship, to dance before the Lord, or to experience the indwelling of the Holy Spirit. I pray that we will remember how David danced joyfully before the Lord without reservation. The Bible speaks so many times of these outward expressions by His people in their worship and praise to the Lord. Then and now, at age 91 as I tell my story, I stand in awe of a loving but powerful God. I believe He is waiting for the day when His people will be free to worship Him as the Holy Spirit leads them and not as tradition dictates. I love to walk and pray and be filled with the Holy Spirit through speaking in tongues. As it was then and remains still, it is the highlight of every day for me.

CHAPTER 4

Africa Calling

O n a particular Sunday morning, I kept hearing the word "Africa," pondering it over and over in my heart. At the time, I did not understand intercessory prayer. What I did understand was how much I loved just spending time with my Savior. His words in the Bible would come alive and He would bring to mind verses that spoke to my heart. Before this, it was hard for me to read His Word, but after coming to know Him as I did, it became my daily bread. I hungered and thirsted for His Word and to dwell in His presence.

> "BLESSED ARE THOSE WHO HUNGER AND THIRST
> FOR RIGHTEOUSNESS, FOR THEY WILL BE FILLED."
> (MATTHEW 5:6)

Sometime after that, my pastor kept talking about Africa during his sermon. Following the service, I told him I felt God had called me to go to Africa. It was amazing how my beliefs as to how God was leading me were affirmed so many times by my pastor. He then said he had met a man from Kenya, named Seth, who was here temporarily in Tulsa with his family and asked if I would like to talk to him. Of course, I did. A few weeks later, Seth visited our church along with his wife and young daughter. While Seth talked to the pastor I visited with his wife, telling her I was going home to Africa with them. Because of God's call to me, I felt Africa *was* my destined home at that time. More visits followed with the family and after a few months, they made the decision I could go with them. I continued going to church faithfully, and on many occasions would go at night to be alone, spending my time walking and praying until morning.

Before going, I knew I had to get a visa and passport, but had no earthly idea how to go about it. God did, however, and in His heavenly wisdom took me to all the right people and places to accomplish the necessary tasks.

The time was drawing near for me to leave. As I was sitting at my desk one day at work, God spoke to me, saying, "Sell your house." Not doubting His words or hesitating this time, I called a real estate agent I knew. He looked at the house, bringing with him a couple he thought would like it and they bought it. God had confirmed His words to me. A few weeks later, after moving out and renting an apartment, God spoke to me with specific instructions to quit my job, give my things away, and to not watch television, pick up my mail or answer my telephone. In order to prepare me for the task laid before me, I felt God did not intend for me to have any distractions, but to use my time in drawing nearer to Him through praise and worship.

Although I didn't fully understand the work He was performing in me, I was obedient in doing all the things He had instructed. I have to admit it was difficult, but still I knew His voice and desired to please Him.

"THEY SOLD PROPERTY AND POSSESSIONS TO GIVE
TO ANYONE IN NEED." (ACTS 2:45)

To me, "anyone in need" applied to the people of Africa. They needed salvation. They needed healing. They needed necessities of life. They needed to know God and He had chosen me as His instrument to minister to those needs according to His divine plan.

When God spoke to me to take His Word to Africa, I naturally thought that I would go there and have the opportunity to personally speak at the churches. Thinking this, an eagerness took root within me and I had God's Word burning inside me with a fervent desire to share it with the African people.

The time finally came for me to leave and I had no idea what lay ahead. I was to meet Seth and his family in Atlanta. I had never flown on a commercial airplane and was completely unaware of where to go or what to do when I got there. My son took me to the airport in Oklahoma City and, while waiting, began to converse with a man also flying to Atlanta who graciously offered to help me. In my eyes, that man was an angel sent from God to watch over and guide me safely to my destination.

After arriving in Atlanta, I could not find my traveling companions. Feeling somewhat exasperated, I finally sat down and started talking to God. My conversation went something like this: "God, I don't know why I am going to Africa, but I'm going. You *promised* to be with me. Now, where *are* those people?" Just as it came time for me to board the plane, they arrived. Coincidence? God doesn't deal in coincidences. Nothing ever happens by accident with Him. He was and is and forever will be. He was beside me all the time.

When we arrived in Nairobi, Kenya and stepped off the plane, I was in for quite an unexpected surprise. Everywhere I looked, there were only black people. For this to be a surprise to me only shows how little thought I had actually given as to *anything* concerning my journey to Africa; except that God told me to go and I was going. Looking back, I can only hope my curiosity (or lack of it) about the people and conditions there reaffirms my complete faith in trusting God when He told me to go. However, to say I did *not* experience any anxiety or apprehension upon arrival would be naïve and untrue. It suddenly dawned upon me that Seth and his family were the only people in this entire unfamiliar country that I knew. But even having these feelings, I still relied on the never-failing protective hands of God.

Looking at my surroundings, I understood why God had instructed me before leaving to give up television, mail service and the telephone. It was apparent I would have none of those modern conveniences in Africa. We might consider it living in a vacuum in America to be without all the things we consider necessities. But God, in His infinite wisdom, had removed these things beforehand to prepare me for what I was to now encounter. As we learn from reading His Word, and as we have heard recited so many times, "God does not call the qualified...he qualifies the called." In other words, He had qualified me to live without what many now consider necessities, and to rely solely on Him and His protective promises.

God's given Word to my heart was burning within me. I longed to share it with the people of Africa. I longed for them to know the God that I knew and loved. He opened doors for us and we began going to different churches. The people were very warm and welcoming, but the door of opportunity for me, personally, to actually speak His Word was not immediately opened.

Every morning, I would read my Bible and go for a walk, always praying in the Spirit and praising the Lord. I still had no knowledge of how to find my way anywhere. One particular day, I walked for more than two hours before I finally returned. Upon arriving, I marveled to the Lord how I had not gotten lost, nor was I the least bit tired. When reflecting on this, especially about not being tired, I still love what God spoke to me that day: "I know...I carried you."

During my stay in Nairobi, there were times we had no food, except for rice, rice and more rice; however, I did not feel hunger. Just as when I walked for so long and did not feel tired, God removed the hunger. During this time, I met a lady who sold oranges. Even though we had a language barrier, we had one word we exchanged when we saw each other: "Hallelujah!" You see, hallelujah is the same in every language, and because of this sisterhood in praising God, she would sometimes give me an orange. I am sure this was a sacrifice on her part since this was her way of earning her livelihood, but she shared anyway. It was such a treat after a steady diet of rice. Not only can our Lord turn water into wine, but he can turn an orange into a testimony of how He always provides.

Every morning, I would go out to pray and would see a dog that was noticeably starving. I wanted so badly to feed him, but I could only give him scraps because food was so scarce. One morning, there were not even scraps left over to feed him. As I went out the door, I prayed, "Father, I don't have anything for my dog." As I was going out the gate, there in the street lay a jelly sandwich, which I thankfully gave to the dog. That is the God I serve. He is real and He cares.

> "Are not two sparrows sold for a penny? Yet not one of them will fall to the ground outside your Father's care."
> (Matthew 10:29)

While in Nairobi, I learned people were holding church meetings each day at City Hall. One day while attending, I mentioned to a couple that I had bought a tee-shirt for each of my grandkids and packaged them to mail, but had no idea where the post office was. You can imagine my delight upon discovering the man just happened to work at the post office. He took me there and I presented the package for mailing. The person waiting on me said, "You will have to have a string tied around it before you can mail it." Not having a string or knowing where I was going to get one, I explained to him I simply did not have one. He looked on the floor and there lay a string just long enough for the package. Small miracle, some might say. When you have a need, no miracle is small. Nothing but a string would do at that time for me to be able to mail my package and that's exactly what God provided. I praised Him as if He had provided manna from Heaven. My particular need had been met.

We later started meeting in a hotel on Sunday mornings and evenings to share the Word of God with the people. Several Sundays had passed and one morning, as we were singing and praising God, a young man came into the room. He related he had been in the hotel, sitting at the bar and drinking a beer, when he heard our singing and wondered what it was. He said the Holy Spirit came upon him and he was saved immediately upon hearing it. But when he returned to his room, the Devil said to him, "You are not saved." He said he then reached into the nightstand drawer where he found a Gideon Bible and, upon opening it, the pages fell open to Romans where he read: "Whoever calls upon the name of the Lord shall be saved." He then knew his salvation was real and secure.

You can imagine our surprise upon learning he was a guard for the prince of Swaziland. He wanted to share his testimony about his salvation experience on Sunday night and we were happy to let him do so. He told us when he returned home he was not going to preach to the poor but was going to start at the top with the secretary and top political officials. God put it on my heart to give him my Bible and, when I did, he began to cry like a baby. I called him one day after I had returned home from Africa and he told me he was still following the Lord. The wonder and amazement of God's divine intervention in this young man's life simply overwhelmed me. We never know how God is going to use us to draw people to Him. In this case, it was through our worship singing.

The people of Nairobi did not have trash service or city dumps as we do in our modern world, so they would put their garbage at the end of the streets. You can imagine the sickening litter and foul odors always present. One day as I was in the car with Seth and his family, we passed a garbage pile and I cursed it in the name of Jesus. When we were on the way home later, it was burning. After witnessing this occurrence, Seth told me firmly that I was not to talk or pray with anyone but him. His manner of insistence disturbed me as I was at a loss to understand why he was telling me this.

Following this incident, I was at a noon meeting one day and Seth's assistant walked up, took me by the arm and said Seth had told him to bring me home. I was not ready to leave and told him I would leave after the meeting. He replied impatiently, "you are going right now." I knew there was nothing to eat when we got to Seth's house, so I told him I was going to get something. He then replied, "No, you can eat at home. Seth said to bring you home now!"

After arriving, Seth again emphasized that I was not to talk or pray with anyone except him. Fear immediately came upon me and I became increasingly afraid of this man. I locked myself in my room every night after returning home and avoided him as much as I possibly could. His attitude and his actions toward me were a complete surprise as he had always asked me to pray for the sick at the end of each meeting.

I felt a need to talk to someone, so I called my pastor, Sam Matthews, at my home church in Shawnee and told him of my fears. Following this, and without my knowledge, he contacted a missionary in Nairobi and told him of my circumstances and my fears. The missionary, Winston, contacted me and I told him what had happened concerning Seth and repeated my fears. I then asked him if I could move over to his ministry. He told me jealousy was a big thing there and that, in order to avoid any problems within his own ministry, I would need to move somewhere else for three months before I could join their ministry. I had no idea what to do or where I could move for three months. But once again, my ever watchful Father intervened. One morning, as I was reading my Bible, God led me to Acts 18:9 where the Lord was speaking to Paul by a vision in the night.

> "DO NOT BE AFRAID ANY LONGER BUT GO ON SPEAKING AND DO NOT BE SILENT FOR I AM WITH YOU AND NO MAN WILL ATTACK YOU IN ORDER TO HARM YOU FOR I HAVE MANY PEOPLE IN THIS CITY." (ACTS 18:9)

Knowing God was speaking directly to me through scripture, I was afraid no longer as I knew God was with me. Having no place to go, I remained there—but with the confidence that God would protect me and keep me safe. As the words in a beautiful picture say: "The will of God will never take you where the grace of God will not protect you."

Toward lunchtime at one of our meetings, I recall asking a couple where they would go to eat after the meetings. Their reply was, "We don't eat…we go back to work." I then realized they gave up their lunch hour for praise and worship. I was so embarrassed at my rush to get something to eat, knowing they would go hungry until their evening meal. There is such a contrast between life in America, with our comforts and our set times to eat, compared to the sacrifices these people made to spend time in worship. Perhaps it's because we take that freedom of worship for granted and assume it will always be the way it is now.

I had lunch one day with a lady I had met at one of our church meetings. After eating, we decided to walk through the business area, putting our hands on the different places of business and praying for the owners and employees. One of the businesses we prayed over was a theater. When I returned to Nairobi on a subsequent trip, I found the theater had been turned into a church. Praise God for answered prayer and intervention. One more place of worship had been established.

During this time, for some reason unknown to me, I had a fervent desire to meet with President Moi, but had no idea which buses to take to get to the president's place of residence. In the meantime, I learned a meeting was held at City Hall each day at noon, where the people would have a praise and worship service and someone would share a word from the Bible. When I attended these meetings I would always pray for God's blessings upon the city.

One day, I saw a sign that read "Office of the President." Being in a foreign country and unfamiliar with their government buildings, I thought perhaps they had an office for the president in the city. I walked to the fence surrounding the building and asked God to make a way for me to see the president, as I now realized the Word burning within me was for him. The next day, I went back and prayed again that God would break down all barriers and make it possible for me to see the president. After watching for a while, I noticed people going around to the back and decided to see if I could get in that way. There were soldiers everywhere and I asked one if I could see the president as I had a word from God for him. His answer to me was to come back the next day.

There were only two soldiers there the next day and, after repeating my desire to see the president, one said I needed to see Mrs. Kendee. He told me I should go to the tallest building in the city, search out Mrs. Kendee and she could get me in to see the president. After finally locating the tallest building and finding Mrs. Kendee, she affirmed she could get me in to see him, but that it would take several days because he was so busy. I went back week after week to see her, determined that it was God's will for me to see and talk to the president.

At last, I went on a Friday and she said he was waiting to see me at his office in the capital. I was so happy I was finally going to meet with him and told her I would take a cab to the capital. You can imagine my delight when she said, "No, you do not need to take a cab… the president is sending a car for you." Sure enough, as I arrived downstairs, there was a driver waiting for me with the door open. He drove me straight to the State House and I walked in on a red carpet. See? Not only had God worked everything out for me to see the president, I was receiving the red carpet treatment in doing so.

The secretary told me to wait there, so I sat down, looked around at all the things in the room and marveled at God's amazing grace in bringing this all about. The moment finally came and I was allowed to see President Moi. After introducing myself, I then told him I had a message for him from God. I cannot remember the entire message I gave him, except that the last words were "I will cause it to rain upon your nation."

At that time, a terrible drought had encompassed their land and it was so dry that the wild animals were dying from lack of water and the people could not plant their crops. He accepted the message graciously. I asked if I could pray for him and he said yes. So I went to him, laid my hands on him and prayed. What a wonderful privilege God had made possible; I could not only get in to *see* the president of this nation, but was given the added blessing of praying for him.

It was raining when I walked out of the building. It continued to rain all of Friday night and all day Saturday and Sunday. The long-awaited and long prayed for rain had come and the people began planting. It was a wonderful time of praise to witness God's hand working and a wonderful testimony to the president of Kenya, affirming the miracles of the one true Jehovah God.

It was difficult to bring the men in Africa to the Lord because many of them had several wives and knew if they truly followed Christ, they would have to give up polygamy and have only one wife. Many of the men did not work and the different wives were the sole providers for their families. I am not aware if this is still the practice today, but it was many years ago when I visited Africa.

Before I was to leave for home, I began to wonder how I was going to get to the airport. I told God I did not know the way or which bus to take. I went to the noon meeting as usual, and upon returning, got on the wrong bus. And you can imagine where it took me—to the airport. God had shown me which bus to take.

One day before I left to come back to the United States, I walked down to a small lake and was worshiping the Lord. As I turned to walk home, I heard the Lord speak to me, "My daughter, I love you and no demon from Hell can take you from me." Once more, the Lord was assuring me that, no matter what I was to encounter in my ministry for Him, all things were according to His will. I knew I need not fear anything for His presence would always be with me.

Chapter 5

Rest & Renewal

When it came time for me to return home, I was talking to the lady at the airport about my ticket. She told me they were having a contest and said I should enter. I filled out the entry form and, upon checking later, found I had won a ten-day first-class trip for two to the Netherlands. I invited a friend, Julie, to go with me. What a wonderful trip it turned out to be. In my heart, I felt God had provided a time of refreshment, rest and renewal for me.

When I say the trip was first class, that is not an exaggeration. We were met at the airport by a limousine, which took us to a nice hotel where we stayed for five days. While there, we decided we wanted to visit The Hague so I contacted a man there who had visited our church back home. He had given us his phone number in case we were ever in the Netherlands. He was glad to hear from us and met us at our hotel. When we got off the train at our destination, we walked along the North Sea. It was very pretty and there were many people enjoying the beach. Much to our astonishment, the women were all bare-breasted. You might say they were incredibly immodest and we were incredibly shocked and somewhat embarrassed.

Afterwards, our host took us to where he and his wife lived in an apartment house on the 4th floor. As there were no elevators there, we walked the four flights of stairs and were out of breath when we reached their floor. Our host introduced us to his wife and I asked her if I might use the restroom. She then took me into a room with a daybed and closed the curtains, thinking I wanted to rest. I was amused and said "No…I need to use the bathroom." She then escorted me to a room that had only a bathtub, thinking I wanted to take a bath. I then recalled they referred to a restroom as a water closet. We finally conquered the language confusion, and at long last, I arrived at my sought after destination.

After leaving the apartment, we walked on a path that looked something like brick, but wasn't. Our host informed us that Alexander the Great was the one who had ordered the walkway constructed. You can imagine the wonder of realizing we were actually walking on a street or pathway which was thousands of years old.

While there, Julie and I also went on a tour and one of our stops was a place where there were acres and acres of beautiful tulips. Words cannot describe what a breathtaking scene we encountered. As we gazed in wonder, we recalled the song "Tiptoe Through the Tulips," and laughingly sang and danced out the lyrics. Windmills covered the countryside and it appeared they were all still very much in use, pumping and supplying water.

The Netherlands is below sea level and is one of the cleanest countries I have ever visited. The people there even wash their livestock. I saw so many black and white cows and it was amazing how white the white was, even considering they are on the outside, roaming and grazing. The houses were lined with gardens full of colorful and beautiful flowers and many had flower-filled window boxes. It was obvious the people took a great deal of pride in preserving the beauty of their land.

We also visited the Soldier's Cemetery. Keeping in mind that this was a nation where a large majority of the population were seemingly godless, and appeared to live accordingly, we stared in wonder at the hundreds and hundreds of crosses lining the grave sites. We asked ourselves: In a nation that is so secular, saturated with drugs, prostitution and nudity, what did the cross represent to them? To us, as Christians, it represents love, purity, and righteousness bought by the shed blood of Christ. It would be interesting to learn the significance of what the cross represented to those who were unbelievers.

After our five-day stay at the first hotel, a limousine arrived once more and we were taken to an old castle for a five-day stay. To say we were thoroughly enjoying it would be an understatement. We were surrounded by its historical authenticity and soaked up the "olden days" atmosphere. Before our five days were up, the manager came by one day and said we were going to have to move to a hotel because the diamond companies were having a convention and they needed our room. Julie and I were very disappointed at leaving our surroundings, and as we were packing, I sat down and said "Julie, God brought us to this place. God wanted us at this place so we are not going to leave." All of a sudden, the manager came in and said "Ladies, one of the men is sick and we are not going to need this room." Rejoicing in God's intervention, I made the remark to Julie it would be nice before we returned home if we could go to one more nation.

The morning we were to fly out, the air traffic controllers all went on strike so we were bussed from the Netherlands to Brussels, Belgium. Although it was just a stop on our way home, God had listened. I had expressed a desire to go to another nation and he took us there, even though it was a short stay. Some might say "Just how much do you think God should intervene on your behalf when you desire something?" I think I am safe in saying "As long as it is in His will, then I think He will intervene until His divine mercy and provision runs out."

> "OH, GIVE THANKS TO THE LORD, FOR HE IS
> GOOD! FOR HIS MERCY ENDURES FOREVER."
> (PSALM 136:1)

So my answer is: Forever.

CHAPTER 6

Back to Africa

Upon my return home, I had no job, no car and no permanent home, but I kept believing and praying, knowing God would show me what to do. One day while at the back of the church praying, God told me to go back to Africa. At the same time, without my knowledge, my pastor, Sam Matthews, and his wife, Kathy, were at the front of the church praying. He called to me and said God had placed it on his heart to buy me a ticket back to Africa. Isn't God's timing wonderful?

> "THERE IS A TIME FOR EVERYTHING, AND A SEASON
> FOR EVERY ACTIVITY UNDER THE HEAVENS."
> (ECCLESIASTES 3:1)

Upon learning I was going back to Africa, I called Winston, the missionary in Nairobi, and told him I was coming back to Africa and asked if I could stay there with his ministry. You can imagine my relief and joy when he said I could come and stay with them since it had now been three months. God had provided a place for me to stay.

Before I arrived back in Kenya for the second time, God spoke to me and told me to stop in Amsterdam for seven days, walking the land and praying. It was there that I met a young lady who had been a "window girl" which, in that country, is another word for prostitute. We were living at the missionary house; my room was next to hers and we became friends. She had accepted Christ as her Lord and Savior and her enthusiasm and excitement was a joy to behold.

After leaving Amsterdam and returning to Africa, I received a letter from her. She wrote that her father had been very ill with cancer and told how sad she had been when she would go to the hospital and see her father lying there suffering and crying. She went on to tell of a particular day when she walked in his room and heard him crying out to God. She had pled the blood of Jesus over him and her father had been saved.

When she returned to the hospital later, she found her father completely healed and putting on his clothes. Her letter was full of praise and love for the Savior and of the miracles He had performed, both in her life and the life of her father. He had become a new creature in Christ and was a totally renewed, strong father. He told her how he enjoyed the rising sun and all of God's creations, and how beautiful he felt inside. It was like the joy she felt was pouring forth from her heart to mine as I read. It was plain to see her newfound faith was touching the lives of everyone around her. How thankful I am to God that I was allowed to be a part of her new life and love for Christ. To see a young lady, once steeped in sin, become a young lady in love with the Lord and walking in the paths of righteousness.

> "THEREFORE IF ANY MAN BE IN CHRIST, HE
> IS A NEW CREATURE: OLD THINGS ARE PASSED
> AWAY; BEHOLD, ALL THINGS ARE BECOME NEW."
> (2nd CORINTHIANS 5:17)

Arriving back in Kenya for the second time was a delight. My routine was the same…walking and praying. My love for the people God put on my heart the first time was just reaffirmed and I felt better equipped for whatever task He laid before me. I stayed in the home of the missionaries, Winston and his wife, Rita. She received a phone call one day from another woman asking her to come and pray for her. Rita asked if it was alright if I came with her and the lady agreed that I could.

When we arrived at the lady's home, to my surprise, it was the same lady who had made the arrangements for me to meet with the president of Kenya. She stated doctors had told her she had cancer of the uterus. I laid hands on her and prayed and God immediately healed her. Her sister was also there and said she had been suffering from back problems. After praying for her, she was also immediately healed. Word spread quickly of their healing.

One night as I lay in bed reading my Bible, I heard a knock on the door and it was a young lady asking me to come and pray for her father who had suffered a stroke, leaving his left side paralyzed. I went to their home and prayed for him. She later told me he had been healed and was off all his medication.

"BUT HE WAS WOUNDED FOR OUR TRANSGRESSIONS;
HE WAS BRUISED FOR OUR INIQUITIES; THE
CHASTISEMENT OF OUR PEACE WAS UPON HIM; AND
WITH HIS STRIPES, WE ARE HEALED." (ISAIAH 53:5)

A few days later, I received an invitation to the president's garden party, which was an amazing honor. Upon arriving, a gentleman approached me and asked if I was a dignitary. I said "no," but later thought, "I'm a child of the King," and should have said so. They sat me on the very first row, and after the party, the president shook hands with everyone on the front row. As he approached, I asked God to give me a word for the president, and just before the president came to me, I heard the Father say "And it shall come to pass." When he shook my hand, I said "The Father said 'It shall come to pass,'" and he warmly shook my hand again.

Invitation to president's garden party

The program was beautiful with dancers dressed in their native tribe's costume. The colors were amazingly bright and beautiful and each dance was unique in its own way. I considered it quite an honor to be invited to the president's garden party and felt God had arranged this enjoyable evening for my relaxation, and for the opportunity once again to witness to the president about God's presence in our lives.

One day at City Hall, after the speaker had given the invitation, I noticed a young man sitting behind me. I was moved to go and talk to him. I asked him if he would like to receive Jesus as His Lord and he answered he would. I led him in the sinner's prayer and he accepted Christ. He shared with me that he had come to town to buy a rope and hang himself but had heard the singing in City Hall and came to see what was happening.

He came back the next day and I bought him a Bible. In reading the Bible after getting home, he said he came across the scripture where Jesus said he was the Light of the world. Later that night as his family sat in the darkness with no light, he spoke to Jesus, saying, "Jesus, your Word says you are the Light," and he said the whole room lit up then as though it were day. His little girls joyfully got up and started playing. It was an unforgettable experience for their family.

The next day, he brought his wife to the meeting and she also received Jesus. They invited me to come to their home for a visit and have bread and tea. The day I decided I should go, we rode the bus for miles, and after getting off, walked across a field. I discovered they lived in one room made of metal with only one door and no windows. I understood after standing in the room what really happened that night when their darkened room became illuminated by God's presence.

They had a small fire in the middle of the room where the wife made tea. She brought out a loaf of bread and we drank tea and broke bread. It was a very moving experience. They had three little girls and I took each of them a doll. All little girls love dolls and they were no exception. I also took the man's wife a dress. It was so joyful to spend time with this family, realizing what a difference God had made in their meager lives with their newfound faith. Seeing the transformation of this wonderful little family made me so glad that God allowed me to be a part of it.

The miraculous healing which God was bringing about continued. Later, a lady who lived about six blocks away sent for me to come and pray for her newborn baby who had a badly infected umbilical cord. I prayed over the baby, and the next day, two little girls came to tell me the baby was healed and the umbilical cord had come off. God is so good. Every day, His power was evident in so many lives.

The lady who had arranged for me to see the president and had been healed told me she knew God had used *her* to get me in to see the president, and in turn, had used *me* by bringing me back to Africa so that she could be healed. Lives intertwined for the glory of the Lord.

CHAPTER 7

Weeping Over India

After returning from Africa the second time, I was at church praying and heard "INDIA." I told Brother Sam, my pastor, I knew God was calling me to go to India. As always, my pastor said he would pray about it. I knew I could rely on his prayers.

As I was praying one day in the spirit, I began to cry. Time held no meaning as I sobbed. When I finally quit, I realized I had been crying for an hour and didn't know why. A prophet visited our church later, came up to me and said "Grace, the Father said to tell you that you will cry over India like He cried over Jerusalem." How my heart rejoiced. I knew then why I had cried. God was preparing me for what I would experience in India. Having no idea as to when or how I would get to India, I knew God had told me to go and relied on Him to provide the way.

As it happened, a few days later friends of the pastor, Bob and Ruth Stay, were on their way to Dallas to see their son and his family and he said it just came to his mind to stop and visit with Brother Sam. They had not seen each other for quite some time. In visiting together, he shared with Brother Sam that he and his wife were going to India in a few weeks with a group of about twelve. Brother Sam told him he had a lady in his church who was an intercessor and God had told her to go to India. Brother Sam asked if I could go with them. You can imagine my excitement and enthusiasm after Pastor Stay contacted the leader of the group and obtained permission for me to go. Once more, God had secured my way to where He was leading me.

After going through all the preparations, the time came to leave and, after hours of flying, we landed in what was then Bombay, India. After arriving, we sadly learned the leader of our group would not be permitted to stay in the country with us as he had been caught on his previous visit baptizing people into the Christian faith. We learned natives in India can baptize each other, but outsiders are not allowed to do so. It was so disappointing for him and his wife and for our group when they had to return home, but our mission still lay ahead of us.

Our remaining group then took a train to Warangal. The plan was to stay in a church there, but since they were not prepared for us when we arrived, we stayed in a hotel for about a week. The first evening, we learned that a cafe was in the basement of the hotel so we decided to have dinner there. We were surprised and happy to learn that the cafe offered Mexican food and so that's what we all ordered. As we waited for our food, someone turned to look at the table behind us and there were three huge rats on the table eating the scraps. When the waiter saw the appalled look on all our faces, he immediately took his apron and shooed them back into the wall.

We couldn't imagine why he appeared to be protecting rather than exterminating them. Then we remembered in India, no animals were ever killed for the people believe in reincarnation and were always fearful they could be killing a relative or friend. Needless to say, after our visual encounter with the rats, we all decided to forgo the Mexican food and went on a fast.

My roommate at the hotel was an eighteen year old girl named Beth. One day when we left our room, we unknowingly left the window open. That was a mistake. While we were out, a monkey came through the open window, ate all our cookies, jumped up and down on our bed and tore our sheets in shreds. The chaos was unbelievable. Perhaps a similar situation led to the line "No more monkeys jumping on the bed" in the children's song "Five Little Monkeys." We made *sure* we always closed the windows after that.

After a week or so, the church was ready for us to move in. Our rooms were separated by hanging quilts between the beds, which consisted of one-inch mattresses on the floor. Our routine began each day with Ruth and I cooking breakfast which, most of the time, was scrambled eggs. The natives there would cook our lunches, consisting mostly of rice and vegetables. For dinner, we would eat leftovers from that day's two previous meals. When in poverty-stricken countries like India, we were thankful we had enough to eat and didn't spend a lot of time wishing for something better.

For our meetings in Warangal, we met on a platform made of many small sticks which, from their appearance, would not be strong enough to hold us. However, through God's power, the platform *always* remained in place. The people would start coming as soon as they heard the music. Usually, we would have approximately 1200 to 1500 each night. Oxcarts would arrive full of people curious to see what was occurring.

Stick platform

We noticed the same people would come forth every night when the invitation was given. They didn't seem to understand that the creator of all things was the one and only true God and that His wonderful plan of salvation did not require coming forward nightly. They worshiped so many gods, each representing different things. I observed one man bow down and worship an ox. It was such a sad sight to see, but the people had been steeped in the concept of many gods in many forms and it was not easy for them to forsake all these generations of false teaching.

A lady came forward at one of the meetings and accepted Jesus Christ as Lord of her life and asked us to pray for her protection. She said when her husband found out, he would either kick her out of the house or kill her. She had a small baby in her arms and the thought of what she faced was heartbreaking, but we had no way of keeping her safe, except to plead the blood of Jesus over her. How blessed we are in America to have the freedom of accepting Christ. We are either not aware, or fail to remember, there are so many people who face persecution or death for that wonderful experience.

CHAPTER 8

Demonic Presence

E very night the demons would manifest themselves in different forms. We saw people get down on the ground, slithering and twisting their bodies like snakes. Others would vomit and let out terrible screeching manifestations because of their awareness and fear of the presence and power of Jesus. Anyone who doubts Satan is still the prince of this world and roams about seeking whom he can destroy should witness events such as these. A lost soul could do nothing but tremble at these fearful sights and sounds. Hallelujah for the blood of the lamb that is greater than he that is in the world. Instead of trembling in fear, believers can rejoice for this divine assurance.

At the end of each meeting, people who were sick or had been touched by God were invited to come forward. Each had the opportunity to give their testimony as to how God had worked in their lives and hearts that night. We always prayed for the healing power of Jesus for those suffering and ill, and saw God's hand at work in so many ways.

For some reason, I was put in charge of going to the markets and buying the food for our group. I remember so well when I was at an open market and I heard someone say, "Ox Ox!" I turned immediately to see a huge ox behind me. I knew from past experience that the ox had the right of way and I moved out of the way quickly and allowed the ox to pass. Their belief prevented touching or harming the ox in any way.

On another occasion, I wanted to pet a donkey but was prevented from touching it in any way as the people believed it might be someone's relative or friend. What a heartbreaking thought it was to know that in this country people were starving for lack of food when life-saving animals fit for consumption were roaming all around, protected because of the pagan beliefs of the people.

The conditions in these villages were grossly unsanitary. Open sewers were everywhere and the odor was overwhelming. Pigs living in these sewers were referred to as "sewer hogs," and of course, these animals were also off limits as a food source. How strange to observe how the animals took precedence there over humans in so many ways.

After about three weeks, we left Warangal and rode a bus to Bidar. The only air conditioning was open windows and it was unbearably hot. We stopped at Hyderabad for lunch, which was a refreshing reprieve. The people there spoke English and we enjoyed the good times and laughing with ones that we could actually understand and with whom we could have a coherent conversation. In Bidar, we stayed at a school, and once more, had to put benches together for beds.

Beds in Bidar

We had no stove to cook on for several days. Bob Stay had a two-cup coffee maker and we hit on the idea of boiling eggs in the coffee maker and it worked! Imagine that! A luxury...boiled eggs. All the shops closed in the afternoons because of the extreme hot temperatures, so we had to make sure we purchased everything we needed before they shut down. We quickly adjusted to doing without 24-hour grocery supercenters.

CHAPTER 9

God Says "Go Home"

One day I was out walking and praying and God spoke to me, saying, "Go home." My first thought was I had done something which was not pleasing to Him. I told the others and Bob Stay jokingly said "Yes, you were out *praying* for God to send you home." Still, the hurt remained until the next morning when my son called. It was a miracle even to be able to receive a phone call from Oklahoma to India. Since I was close to the phone, I answered it. I was so surprised and excited when I heard my son's voice, but saddened when he said "Mother, come home. Your sister, Polly, is dying of cancer."

Although the news was heartbreaking, I then knew I had the freedom to return home. I no longer felt guilty wondering if I had displeased God. I understood why the Father had told me to go home. Later, as I was out praying and thanking Him, He said "I will bring you back," and I knew I could pack and leave for home with His blessing. The Stay's decided to leave with me. My sister only lived one month after I returned, but I was so thankful and blessed God allowed me to spend those last days with her.

During many of my trips, I must admit that I would get homesick, missing my sons and loved ones and longing to see them. The opportunities to contact them were very limited. I felt sometimes they didn't really understand my journeys and extended times away from them. Perhaps I should have communicated my feelings more in helping them to understand, but I didn't know how to convey my feelings to them. I just knew when God speaks to you and you know in your heart He is telling you to go and preach Christ to a lost world, obeying Him becomes your utmost desire. Christ tells us when we choose to follow Him, He must become the most important thing in our lives and we must be willing to leave father, mother, and loved ones. There is no assurance, however, we won't miss them. I had to depend on God to fill the void of being away from those I loved. I still remain dependent on Him to this day to fill that void when I'm away.

CHAPTER 10

Going to Ghana

After returning from India, I received a call from the missionary, Winston, telling me they had begun a ministry in Accra, Ghana and he invited me to join them. I sought the Lord's will in much prayer, and after doing so, felt God wanted me to be a part of the ministry at its beginning. After making the decision, I wrote Winston letters detailing my flight number and time of arrival. Thankfully, God provided for me financially in order for me to make the trip. To my surprise, no one was there to meet me when I arrived. Once more, I was in a strange place knowing no one. The letters I had sent to Winston previously were sent to a box number only so I had no physical address and no idea how to locate him.

I looked around for some time in an effort to find someone to help me. Finally, a young man walked up and asked if he could help me fill out the mandatory papers I held in my hands, which were required upon arrival. I explained to him my problem; I had just arrived from America and the person that was supposed to meet me had not shown up. He said his friend had a car and they would take me to a missionary house. As I had not felt led by God to stay at a missionary house, I asked them to take me to the closest motel instead. After checking in, I went straight to my room, feeling admittedly a little concerned and alone. Knowing the Holy Spirit was with me, I put a pillow on the floor, got down on my knees and prayed.

The next morning, an employee came to the door and asked if he could bring my breakfast. I gladly agreed he could. I had learned after years of missionary work and missed meals not to pass up the opportunity to partake when food is offered. After eating, I went to the office and told my story to the desk clerk. She told me I should take a cab to the post office and put a note in the people's post office box to let them know where I was staying.

As I left, a cab driver walked up and asked if he could help. It was always so wonderful the way God provided so many people in so many walks of life offering to assist me. I repeated my story to him and he told me he would take me to the post office, which was outside the city. We drove along the ocean and it was a breathtakingly beautiful site, reminding me the same God who had created the oceans would take care of me.

After getting to the post office and relaying my story once more, the lady working there told me to put a note in the box, informing Winston of my whereabouts. I did and then returned to the motel. Upon arriving and asking the fare, the cab driver said he was not going to charge me. Blessed again, I went back to my room and began to pray. As soon as I did, I heard a knock on my door, and upon opening it, was overjoyed to see that it was Winston, the missionary. He was a very welcome sight. He told me he had *just received* my first note telling the details of my flight number and arrival date, and upon realizing I had probably already arrived, had gone to the airport in an effort to find me. The night clerk just happened to be there and told him she remembered an American lady had come in the night before. He knew I had arrived, but still had no idea where I was at that point. Upon going by to check his post office box, he found my note and came straight to the motel.

As we left and I went to pay for the motel and breakfast, the bill came to exactly $50. The couple from Shawnee who took me to the airport in Oklahoma City to leave for Ghana had told me at the time they felt led to give me $50. Not $45…not $60…but $50. God knew and had provided.

> "But my God shall supply all your need according to his riches in glory by Christ Jesus." (Philippians 4:19)

The roads in Ghana were in terrible shape and because of their deteriorated condition, we would have to park a long distance from the homes and walk. We learned the bad road conditions were because a coup had taken over sometime before and had changed the currency, making the people's money worthless. They could not even buy bread or other food. Fruit trees and homegrown gardens were their only source of income and sustenance. The economy in all areas was suffering.

After getting settled in at the home of Winston and his wife, Rita, I felt led to walk and pray every morning after breakfast, and as I did, met so many people along the way. The love of God in my heart was overwhelming for the land and its people. How do you pray for an entire nation? It is beyond me so my answer would have to be to just yield that heartfelt love, concern and compassion to the Holy Spirit, and He does the rest.

Winston and family

Each night, we would hold prayer meetings in the homes of the people. It was a joy for me to be accepted and welcomed in such a personal way. I shared God's love and His plan of salvation whenever and wherever I could, planting the seeds and depending on God to bring forth harvest, according to His Word. In addition to walking and praying, I felt led to dance before the Lord in our services. It wasn't long before the churches followed in dancing and worshiping the Father.

One day as we were out walking, I saw two young boys with sticks chasing a rat and hitting it. I couldn't understand why and asked Winston about it. He told me that in Ghana rats, and even bats, were included in their diets and they were probably going to take it home for their next meal. In a country so poverty-stricken and food so limited, it was understandable, knowing it was necessary in many cases to avoid starvation. I thought of the verse in the Bible (Acts 10:15) where the Lord told Peter not to call anything unclean which God had made.

While in Ghana, I learned quickly that in the country of Suriname, the blacks and Indians did not like each other. There was a young lady there from Suriname and we discovered her father had told her not to marry a black man and not to come home if she did. One of the leaders of the church was a young black man and he said God had told him his wife would come from a foreign country.

As it happened, the young black man fell in love with this young Suriname lady but she rejected him over and over. Although the young man expressed to her and to us that he felt it was God's will that he marry her, she continued to resist. We were all in agreement with his feelings about God's will for his life and we related our feelings to her. Still, she refused to listen to what God was saying. Afterwards, she became so ill she was bedridden. Nothing we did or said seemed to affect her and she was not improving.

As I was out praying one day, God said to go tell her if she would obey Him, He would raise her up. I told her what God had said. After she failed to get any better, she finally accepted God's Word. After her decision was made, she was healed immediately, rose up from her bed, walked into the kitchen and announced she was going to marry the young man. They were married a short time later and remain happily married to this day with several children. This was another affirmation of the amazing results when we listen, believe and obey God's voice.

God was always present at our meetings and it was wonderful. We sometimes forget what we have in Christ—sent to bring salvation to a lost world. What love the Father has shown.

Going home one day, I observed so many houses unfinished as if they had run out of money to complete them. Walking and praying, I began to prophesy. In my spirit, I saw completed houses and roads. I heard from the people after I returned home and it was unbelievable as to how God had blessed them. Many houses and highways had been completed and I learned they had discovered oil in their country, providing the financial resources needed to rebuild. I felt it was fulfillment of the prophecy God had given me.

While in Ghana, I noticed bumper stickers about God on some of the cars. One day, God said "They know about me, but they don't know me." It was so true. I thanked God I had been given the opportunity to minister to them.

The time came when I felt I should return home. However, the people wanted me to stay another month and I agreed. Since I thought I had bought my ticket for only one month, I knew it would be necessary to have my ticket extended. In going to the airport to do so, I learned that when the clerk had written it out originally, she had mistakenly made it out for two months. For some reason, however, the officials kept my passport and said I would get it back when it was time for me to leave.

When the time was growing close for my departure, Winston started going by the airport each day to pick up my passport, and each time, they would tell him to come back the next day. The day before I was to leave, they told him I would have to come in myself and pick it up. God had already told me that day Winston was on his way to come get me, so I was ready when he arrived.

When I walked into the office, a man was waiting for me at a large desk with a big cigar in his mouth, looking a little bit unnerving. He began to question me about why I was there and I told him my Father had told me to come and pray for this nation. He asked, "your Father?" I replied, "Yes, God is my Father." He almost dropped the cigar out of his mouth, but continued questioning me and writing as he did. I asked him why he was writing and again asked for my passport. He sent for it and when he did, I asked if I could come back to his country again. He replied, "Yes, you are always welcome." I took my passport and left. I still have no idea as to the delay of my passport and the questioning which took place, but I do know it was in God's hands and all things worked out to my benefit once more.

CHAPTER 11

From Ghana to Nairobi

After leaving Ghana, I went through Nairobi and spent a month with the Helseth family whom I had met previously through my church home. Major Helseth, his wife, Lucie, and their children lived in Nairobi where he was stationed at the U.S. Embassy. I had contacted them upon learning I was going to Nairobi and they graciously invited me to stay with them while there.

After arriving, the Helseth family decided to go on a camping trip, and after much persuasion, convinced me to go with them and their children. This was my first camping trip and I was somewhat unprepared for what followed. We camped in the mountains and it was evident by the smell in our camping area that the lions had been there marking their territory. Needless to say, I made sure I stayed close to our campsite and did not wander far away. All our cooking was done over a campfire. Lucie had bought eggs for our trip, and before leaving, had broken them into a jar. This would prevent them from becoming broken on the way. When it came time to cook them, she would pour them out of the jar, one at a time. It's amazing the many smart ideas they had learned after going on so many camping trips.

One of our hopes while there was that we would be able to see some wild animals, but not too close. We didn't have much luck until it was time to go home and we spotted a herd of elephants with their babies. They were huge and as they stomped through the forest, they pushed down trees as they traveled. It was plain to see how a herd of animals could destroy crops as it was impossible to build fences sufficient to hold them back.

After speaking one day at the noon meeting, a lady walked up to me and said she was the sister of Mrs. Kadee, the one whose back was healed. She asked me if I would like to go see Mrs. Kadee. I did, so we made arrangements for me to spend the night at her house. On the way, her sister told me there was a minister of the government coming to see me at Mrs. Kadee's home. Upon arriving and visiting for a while, the minister of the Transportation Agency came and began asking me questions about God, how I had gotten there and about my faith in the gospel reaching his land. He was noticeably upset as he told me people were coming into the State House and leaving items that had been cursed to come against President Moi and as he talked, he began to cry.

Many people in Nairobi believed in and practiced voodooism and witchcraft. I prayed with the minister and as I did, I felt the love, holiness and power of God in our presence. I shared these feelings with him in the hope it would be an encouragement to him. After visiting for a while, we went back to Mrs. Kadee's sister's home. They asked if I would write a letter to the president, telling him I was back in his country and still praying, standing and believing for the salvation of his people. I was glad to do so.

During our stay, Major Helseth would preach at different churches and I was so blessed by going with them and praying over the children. He asked me on one occasion if I had anything to say and I shared with them a message God had given me from Exodus 23, verses 20–30. After delivering it, the people said the message had already been confirmed to them by God. It was so wonderful to know God had prepared the people's hearts for His message.

CHAPTER 12

Remembering Russia

After returning home, the Helseths gave me the opportunity to stay in a house close to my church home which they had purchased. They allowed me to stay there rent free. What a blessing. It felt so good to be able to start attending my church and see all my friends there. I remained in the Helseth house for several years between my various trips.

Before I had gone to India, I had been praying at the church and heard "Russia," so I knew one day I would go there and God would provide the way.

One of the people I had gone to India with on my first trip was a Dr. Jonathan from Birmingham, Alabama. After I had been home for a while, our church held a conference, and surprisingly, Dr. Jonathan was in attendance. In asking him what was next in his life, he replied he was getting ready to go to Russia. He related he had a partner with him in his practice in Birmingham and the two of them would take turns going on mission trips and it was his turn to go. I asked him if it would be possible for me to go with him to Russia. I was so happy when he said I could.

In order for me to be prepared to leave in time, he gave me the name of a certain lady to call to rush my visa. This was such a relief as visas and passports can sometimes be met with so many obstacles, but with her help, I was successful in obtaining it. We met in New York where we joined up with a couple from Florida and a young man from Birmingham. The doctor made all the arrangements for our trip, including hotels, places we would visit and our flight.

Our first stop was Moscow, where Dr. Jonathan had a bus waiting for us. We decided to visit Red Square before going to our hotel. When we arrived there, it was so cold I passed up the opportunity to see the sites and remained on the bus. I have always had an aversion to extremely cold weather. Sometimes I wonder if the aversion is my thorn in the side, except I get cold all over.

We were so grateful the doctor had received all the necessary permissions and requirements for our ministry beforehand. One day we decided we would go to a school to see if we could minister to the students. Dr. Jonathan talked to the person in authority and we were given the proper permission. We went to the auditorium where all the students and teachers had gathered. Dr. Jonathan took Bibles which he had brought with him to the auditorium and presented a message about Jesus, the Christ, and then asked if anyone would like a Bible. Every student and teacher there asked for and received a Bible. It was such a blessing to see their response, especially in the country of Russia.

We also visited hospitals where Dr. Jonathan would minister to the doctors and nurses while we ministered to the patients. Sometimes during the day, the others would go and minister at different locations but I felt it was my calling on those occasions to walk and pray while they ministered. During our two weeks in Russia, we traveled to many different cities, staying in various hotels. All the modern conveniences were available at the hotels, but at 10PM the water was turned off. We learned quickly and not too happily that anything requiring water better be completed before that time as it wasn't turned back on until morning.

In visiting one hospital, we discovered the second floor was only for children with cancer. The entire floor was full and the doors were open in every room. Some of the children were out playing, but the ones who were too sick to play remained in their rooms. It was overwhelming and heartbreaking to see all the little children stricken with cancer. All we could do was love them and pray for them. The children received us gladly and openly and it was a joy to be able to bring them some degree of comfort.

When eating in a restaurant, we noticed we were always served cucumbers. We never discerned what the importance of cucumbers was to every meal, but to be on the safe side of not offending them for any reason, we ate them anyway. When in Rome, do as the Romans do, so to speak, and we decided in that instance, it might be a good rule to follow in Russia, too.

In one city, we handed out pamphlets for the night service and were told the pastor there was an eighteen year old boy. When we arrived for the service, we discovered he was not there. It turned out the boy had undoubtedly done something wrong and his mother had grounded him. I must say it was the first time I had ever attended a service where the pastor had been grounded. Fortunately, the couple from Florida filled in for him and ministered that night. The Holy Spirit spoke during the service and said "I am here to heal," and that night, anyone who came forward experienced the Savior's healing power.

Later that night, I met a Christian lady and she very much wanted me to come to her apartment and pray for God's blessing upon her little home. I was glad to do so and enjoyed being invited inside. I was surprised to learn the lady made whistles and the money received from selling them was her sole source of income. It was the only time while in Russia I was actually invited into someone's home. I never learned why we weren't invited as most countries we traveled in welcomed us, even into the most primitive of abodes.

The architecture of Moscow was beautiful with some of the buildings dating back to the 12th century. The roads were average, but we noticed that all along the highways, there were fences built so high that you could not see what was on the other side. It certainly aroused our curiosity but not enough to venture away from the security of the highways and into the countryside to find out what was behind them.

While in another city, we attended a church where an eighteen year old girl was the pastor. She got up, read from her Bible and then closed the service. Three or four people came forward to receive Jesus. Since we couldn't understand the Russian language, we assumed the Bible from which she read was the same as our King James Version and contained the gospel message since the ones coming forward apparently responded to the salvation call.

When we checked out of the hotel to return to Moscow, an elderly lady was outside selling cards in the bitter cold without a coat. I felt sorry for her and gave her my gloves. The thought came to me to give her my coat, but it was so brutally cold, I decided to keep it as I didn't have the resources to buy another.

It snowed all the way back to Moscow and it was beautiful, but not enticing enough to make me want to get out of the warm bus and play in it.

CHAPTER 13

God Keeps His Promise

After arriving home from Russia, I received a phone call from Bob Stay saying they were returning to India and asked if I would like to join them. How I rejoiced at the news. I had no doubt that since God had told me He would bring me back to India, it was His will that I return.

When we arrived there, we stayed at a doctor's home in Bidar. It was so heartwarming to see the apparent love the doctor had for his people. He would hire different ones to go out into the villages and bring those with leprosy in for treatment. The lepers were basically outcasts and afraid to come in to see the doctor for fear of being mistreated by others. After receiving the proper medical treatment, many recovered.

One day, the doctor took us to a colony of approximately fifty healed lepers. It was so wonderful to witness those who had been healed, but sad to see so many left with their eyes eaten out, as well as some without hands, ears, limbs and other disfigurements. It was so mindful of the days of Christ when the outcast lepers had no hope of healing, except those blessed to be touched with the power of the divine healer.

After visiting with the people there, they insisted with amusement I ride a donkey with a homemade saddle. After much hesitation, I finally agreed. The ride was less than smooth. Even a horse and wagon would've been welcomed at that point. After a short while, and because of my somewhat exaggerated pleas, the ride was terminated. It was apparent from their laughter the onlookers enjoyed the ride much more than I did.

Grace riding donkey in leper colony

Later, a group of the healed lepers gathered in a building and Bob ministered to them through preaching and praying. Every village we visited would greet us with colorful leis, mostly made from wild flowers with sometimes very unpleasant odors. Regardless of the pungent smell, we knew their acts were done in love and appreciation and we accepted them willingly. We arrived unexpectedly a little early at the village one evening and the people asked us to go back out and come in again. When we did, they presented us with leis again, playing music as they gave them to us. It seemed to give them great pleasure to bestow us with these gifts.

The buses there did not run after a certain time in the evening and presented a great inconvenience to the pastor. He would ride the bus to the village services each night, but if the service lasted too long, he would have to walk as much as five miles home as the buses would no longer be running. Bob, Ruth and I talked it over and decided to put our money together and buy the pastor a moped. His excitement at receiving it was a delight to behold. He would now be riding back and forth to his meetings in style. We received a real blessing from being able to make it possible.

On many occasions during the day, I would go up on the roof of the doctor's house to pray and worship God alone without distractions. On one of these occasions as I was worshiping and praising the Lord, the Holy Spirit came and sat down beside me. I was instantly aware of His presence. I did not take a breath or move as I was so humbled and overwhelmed. It was a feeling of such total love, peace and calm that the experience was, and remains to this day, indescribable.

When we left the doctor's home, we traveled to Krishnagiri, which is south of Bangalore. This was a short distance from where Thomas, the disciple, was killed. Church tradition and history, some of it admittedly somewhat uncertain, tells us Thomas traveled possibly as far as India to preach the gospel. This would lead us to believe he overcame the name so often given to him, "doubting Thomas," and instead became a bold witness for Christ. It has also been speculated he was possibly one of the first to bring the gospel to the Far East. While establishing a church in India, he was stabbed with a spear and died. This might explain why he is still considered a patron saint of India. How exciting it is to think a disciple who walked and talked with the Savior still has such a spiritual influence in that country today.

In Krishnagiri, we stayed with a pastor and his wife. We've all heard the expression "Don't drink the water," and we certainly could not there. It was unfit to drink without first boiling it. Because of this, we drank a lot of soft drinks and bottled beverages, and it made me realize there is just no substitute for a good, cold drink of water. While there, the main stay for our diet was rice. Rice, rice everywhere and not a steak in sight. It would be a misleading statement if I said I did not long for one from time to time.

White people were a rarity to the people there. We visited a village one day and were told no white person had ever visited there. It seemed they never took their eyes off us. We wondered if they even heard the message we presented because of their noticeable amazement at the color, or lack of it, of our skin.

Out walking one day, I saw two men with their flock of sheep coming in for the night. There were a great number of them and the sheep were all grazing together without fencing or boundaries of any kind to keep one flock from mixing with the other. When the shepherds were ready to leave, they called, and to my surprise, the sheep started separating on their own, each one returning to their own shepherd. It reminded me of the verse in the Bible that says "And he calls his own sheep by name, and leads them out." It was a moving sight to see; also such a wonderful illustration of our Lord knowing and calling us by name.

A large mountain was in back of the house where we were staying and I asked Ruth one day if she wanted to go to the mountain to pray. We set out to go there but it turned out to be a lot farther than it looked. After much walking, growing more exhausted with each step, we finally decided we were not going to make it to the mountain. As we were returning, we discovered a black baby lamb and its mother in a field. I asked Ruth to watch the mother so I could pick up the baby lamb as I wasn't sure what the mother would do. While holding it, the significance came to me of how each believer, or each little lamb, is precious in the sight of the Lord. These little unexpected experiences, though seeming unimportant to some, touched my heart deeply as I felt God's love revealed in so many ways.

In the town of Krishnagiri where we were, the only mode of transportation the pastor used in that area was a motorcycle. This served the purpose until the rainy season. He very much needed a bicycle then as it was much easier to handle when he had to travel on wet roads to some of the villages. We talked about how much safer it would also be for him, so we pooled our money and bought him one with all the bells and whistles. He was so proud of the more practical and safe transportation and all the trimmings were an extra delight to him. I wonder how many American pastors would be as delighted as he was to receive a bicycle as a love gift. I'm hopeful there are many who would graciously accept any gift offered to them in love.

Before leaving for home, we stayed one night at Bangalore and then traveled to Amsterdam. We stayed with a pastor friend of Bob and Ruth's in Rotterdam ten days for some much needed rest and relaxation. No one was supporting us at that time so I was limited financially. In fact, I was completely out of money. During one of the services, I told the Father I had no money to put in the offering and it bothered me. About that time, a woman just walked from across the room and to my surprise, handed me some money. I accepted it graciously. Not being familiar with the currency system, I had no idea how much it was, but put it all in the collection plate. It may have been pennies from heaven, or perhaps much more, but I knew no matter how great or small, it came from God.

The next few days, the pastor and his wife gave us a tour of the city. Many of the buildings were new as the battles of World War II had destroyed a lot of the cities. While we were in one of the stores, I stopped to look at a scarf. I must have been openly admiring it as a lady walked up and asked if I liked it. I replied "yes," and without hesitating, she paid for it. God takes care of not only our needs, but in many cases, our desires when we obey Him. I still have the scarf these many years later. It's one more treasured reminder of his provision.

CHAPTER 14

Suriname

In 1994, Bob Stay called and invited me to go to Suriname with him and his wife for two weeks. The churches had started a Bible school there and we stayed with the headmaster of the school. Once again, my goal was to walk and pray for the people in that land. Bob held a revival there, which we attended each night. People were there who were bound by Satan. They believed in and practiced witchcraft and voodooism. Each night there would be people vomiting and screaming at the sound of Jesus' name, but God was still victorious and we did see true salvation in some cases.

One night I was out walking and heard music and I asked the head of the school about it and he said the witches were having a meeting. It was so close to us that we could hear it. The music they were playing was loud and had a particularly weird sound. It was frightening to know the witches were meeting so close to where we were. It was a relief to get back to the school.

I enjoyed spending time with the students at the Bible school and shared some of my things I had brought with me, such as makeup and clothing. I gave a bar of soap to one girl and she was so excited. She told me she left hers outside and a cow had eaten it. Cows, as well as other animals, were allowed to roam at will. It seemed the animals there enjoyed more freedom than the people.

The people of Suriname were more advanced in their way of life and accommodations were more modern and comfortable. We did venture into the city *one* time for ice cream. Considering the hot temperatures in India, this was quite a treat.

CHAPTER 15

Belize

After returning home to the Helseth house for a period of time, I was at a church conference when a young lady stood and prophesied, saying, "I told you to go to Belize." Conviction immediately came upon me and I knew God was speaking directly to me. The girl was among a group of young people who were going to Belize on a summer mission trip, so I joined them. Plans were for me to meet a lady and her two daughters in Houston who were also going. My plane was late so she and her daughters went on to Belize.

When I arrived in Houston, I was told my flight was canceled due to mechanical problems. I spent the night in Houston and flew out the next day, not knowing if there would be anybody to meet me. I sat with a young lady who was a missionary to Honduras, and as we were sharing, I told her of my concerns. She invited me to go to Honduras with her, but when the plane landed in Belize, a young man was standing on the roof atop the airport terminal, waving to get my attention. He was a welcome sight and helped me connect with my group. Once more, God had taken a very unsettling situation, as far as I was concerned, and had put everything back into place. While in Belize, I stayed with the lady and her two daughters. Modern conveniences were not commonplace there either. Barrels were used to catch rain water for our showers. It was a little out of the ordinary, but at least there was no worry about the water being too hard.

One day at a meeting, the speaker invited anyone who wanted to receive Jesus to come forth. Two young girls, ages approximately twelve or thirteen, came forward and the speaker asked me to come and lead them in the sinner's prayer. One of the girls spoke English and the other Spanish. After leading the young lady that spoke English in the sinner's prayer, I turned and asked her if she would lead the other young lady in the prayer in her own language. It was wonderful that this young lady had just experienced for the first time how to present Jesus to the natives. It would be so interesting to know whether the girl continued to follow Christ, and if so, how many souls she led to Christ.

In Belize, my calling once more was to walk and pray for the land. One day, we were out walking and came to the place where you enter the country of Guatemala. We went through the entry process and walked over into Guatemala and prayed in the spirit over the land. One more opportunity God had given me to pray and be a witness in another country.

After returning from Belize, I learned a couple from my church was going there to start a school. I expressed interest in returning and after the school had been started, they invited me to come and join them there. They had a daughter and a son that learned the language quickly and were a real asset to establishing the school. Before I left for Belize, the couple contacted me and said they needed a particular car part from America to get their car running. It seems the school and their home were very far removed from any town or city. They were so thankful upon my arrival to see I had brought the much needed car part which, after a little mechanical expertise, had their car running again. We take so many things for granted in America. A quick trip to the nearest auto parts store and we are usually on the road again. Trips to other countries soon makes one realize how convenient and easy life is in the good old USA.

The school was held outside and the heat was so unbearable they had built an arbor to provide shade. There was no air conditioning there like we are so accustomed to in our schools in America. Education under the conditions they suffered called for much endurance. We take so many of our blessings for granted, including the opportunities for learning and education in a comfortable environment.

I learned of one young man who had become a Christian after being witnessed to by someone at the school. After his conversion, he became the headmaster of the school. His ability to speak Spanish was a real asset as he was able to act as an interpreter there. This made it so much easier for everyone involved to understand and communicate. Eventually, his family also became Christians and he began preaching the gospel. There is no way to determine how many souls were saved and lives changed because of the establishment and outreach of this one school.

In the rainy season, we would cross the river in a ferry. On one occasion, I went with the couple who had started the school, along with their children to visit another couple. We stopped to ask a man on the side of the road how to get to their home. The children's father had been proudly practicing his Spanish and haltingly asked the man for directions in what he thought was coherent Spanish. After we drove off, his daughter said, "Daddy, do you know what you said to that man? Instead of asking the man how to go where we were headed, you asked 'Where are we going?'" We all had a good laugh about what the man must have thought.

I stayed in Belize the second time for approximately a month, away from most modern conveniences. Still, the benefits of ministering to the many needs of the various people far outweighed the inconveniences there.

My son, Jerry, called sometime after I returned home, telling me they were building a home and were going to take care of me. He added I would have a room of my own in the new home. You can imagine how thrilled I was, especially upon learning my room would be *pink*, my favorite color. I was so thankful for this blessing.

House in Belize

CHAPTER 16

ISRAEL

n 1998, at a Women's Monthly meeting at the Sunday school teacher's home on a beautiful, moonlit night, we decided to go out in the yard and sing and praise God. All of a sudden, I heard "ISRAEL." I told the ladies about what I had heard. Sometimes when you hear God speak, it's easy to think maybe you didn't really hear Him and you hope for affirmation. For that reason, I wanted them to know, so if I ever became unsure they could remind me of what I had heard. After telling them, they began asking when I was leaving, and at that point, I couldn't answer. Only God knew—I didn't.

So once again, I called my former pastor, Brother Sam Matthews, and told him of my desire to go to Israel as I felt God had called me to go. I asked if he knew someone there I could stay with as I didn't have the money for a hotel. He said there was a man from South Africa who had a tourist agency there, and gave me his number. I called him and he said he had two flats available and I could stay in one of them free. After being assured of a place to stay, I told my church I was going and they raised $600 which they gave me.

Afterwards, a man in the church who knew I was going to Israel came to me and said God told him to make me a staff to take with me. He and his wife were missionaries to Mexico. He fashioned me a beautiful staff from a mimosa tree, which I accepted proudly and gratefully. When I was ready to leave for Israel, I said, "God, I don't know why I am taking this staff, but you gave it to me." On the way to the airport, I became concerned about the restrictions of items on airplanes and said, "Father, I don't know if they will allow this staff on the plane or not, but I am taking it." As I boarded the plane, the stewardess saw it and remarked, "What a beautiful staff," and of course, they provided a place for it. I didn't have to wonder who had arranged that special place.

John, the man from South Africa with whom I spoke, met me when I arrived in Tel Aviv and took me to Jerusalem. John told me there would be people from time to time that would come there on tours and that when they did, I would be asked to let them stay in the flat. After getting settled, he then took me to his church. It was known as Ruth Heflin's Church, named after an American lady who would come from time to time to preach there.

The first day after arriving in Jerusalem, in approximately April or May, there was a sandstorm and the next morning it snowed. What a contrast. Gratefully, the snow cleared the air and made everything fresh and clean. Each day, I walked and prayed. One morning as I went out, it was extremely cold and the thought came to me "It's too cold today." Always being aware of the discomfort of extreme cold, I thought of going back inside. Just then, a little dove landed just a few feet ahead of me and I started following it to the place where I went each day to pray. I felt the dove was God directing me and forgot about the cold as I continued walking and praying, taking my staff as always.

After service the next Sunday, a lady who had spoken asked me to go to the Old City with her. On the way there, she explained where we were and pointed out different sites. The feeling of awe and wonder upon seeing and recognizing these historical places mentioned in the Bible brought a feeling of peace. When we finally returned to the church, she asked if I would like to rest for the evening service and took me to an upstairs bedroom. You can imagine my delight at learning the lady in the bed next to me was a lady from Dallas, Texas, named Jane who had visited my church in Shawnee, Oklahoma. We became great friends and took many tours and excursions together.

In the coming weeks, people from South Africa, Germany, Switzerland and other nations would come for a tour and stay in my flat with me. They would buy food for their meals and would leave their leftovers in the refrigerator, telling me I was free to eat them. I was always invited to share the evening meal with them also. Thankfully, while tourists were there, I never lacked for food.

Fortunately, there was always someone in the group who could speak English, but it was an enjoyable and enlightening experience to hear the many different languages spoken by the others.

John had a lady who cleaned the apartments where I was staying and he asked her one day if she would take me to the Old City. There were so many interesting Biblical sites to see there, including the Upper Room, David's Tomb and the Wailing Wall. When I walked into the Upper Room, the presence of Jesus and the Holy Spirit overwhelmed me and I could hardly stand. The Upper Room is one large area with no place to sit at all. To just be there and know that this was the place where Jesus and His disciples had been gave me such a feeling of peace and wonderment.

The Wailing Wall was another awesome sight. There were scores of people there. I noticed that the ladies were on one side and the men on the other, according to Jewish custom. Some would place notes into the wall and some would weep, but while I was there, all I could do was pray in the Spirit. The Holy Spirit knew what to pray, even when I didn't.

We also visited the Garden of Gethsemane where Jesus prayed with his disciples the night before His crucifixion. His presence was overwhelming in this place also and a feeling of reverence filled my soul. From the Garden, you can see the Eastern Gate, which someday will gloriously open and Jesus will return. The tops of the trees there are still green and alive but the trunks of the trees resemble driftwood. It's my feeling these trees will remain green until Christ returns.

We also visited the tomb of Jesus and the Skull of Golgotha. It is such an amazing sight as the face on it is still so noticeably visible.

We visited a church in downtown Jerusalem where a pastor gave his awe-inspiring testimony. He related that at one time, he had been an addict and during one of his episodes, Jesus came and took him out into the desert for two weeks and taught him the Bible. He said he had never read the Bible before. His wisdom and sincerity in explaining the scriptures was amazing.

I went back several times and listened to his preaching as I loved to hear him teach the Word. I have never seen anyone that looked more like the likenesses we see of Jesus now in so many paintings and pictures than he did. In listening to his testimony, it brought to mind this beautiful verse, which was so true in his experience.

> "CALL UNTO ME, AND I WILL ANSWER THEE, AND SHOW THEE GREAT AND MIGHTY THINGS, WHICH THOU KNOWEST NOT." (JEREMIAH 33:3)

I cannot recall his name as it has been quite some time, but he is pictured on the following page at one of his services.

Pastor who learned Bible in the desert

Some days, we would go to the Old City and instead of riding a bus, we found it was cheaper to hire and ride in a vehicle much like our SUVs. I sat by a young man on one occasion and noticed he was looking at my staff. He said, "Jesus had a staff like that and He's coming back." "Yes," I answered, "He is coming back." He added, "He's coming back and He will tell the truth." I concluded that he meant by telling the truth, Christ would admit He was not the Messiah. I asked him if he went to church and he replied he did not; he attended the Mosque. I didn't ask any further questions because God revealed to me that the man's definition and mine of truth were not the same.

I also met a lady from Ghana and she told me she had led a friend of hers to Jesus who wanted to be baptized but there was no place available. Her friend asked if she could baptize her in the bathtub. She said she was very hesitant at first, but after thinking about it, decided to do it. When her friend came out of the water, her words were "I have never felt so clean and free." The lady who led her to Christ was so filled with joy knowing that a person could be baptized in a bathtub, realizing it wasn't the place that was important, but what the act represented.

Promenade was another place I visited where the Old City, the Dome of the Rock and many other historical sites were visible. I was walking and praying one day and came to a bench and sat down. I said, "God, I would just like to talk to someone who can speak English *clearly*." As always, I had my Bible with me. I opened it, and a young lady walked up to me, introduced herself, and told me she was from Ohio. She sat down beside me and we discussed the Bible in English and had a great visit. As it happened, she was in Jerusalem for the summer and was working at an orphanage. We talked about the love of Jesus and how he brought us to where we were in Jerusalem. It was so wonderful how God knew I was lonely and needed someone to fellowship with and just share Christ.

Once, while walking and praying with my staff, I said, "Father, Moses had a rod and Aaron had a budding rod. What is the one I have?" God spoke to me and said, "It's a Rod of Grace."

Whenever I attended a service in any location, I always wanted to put money in the collection plate. I had $10 of American money put back in my billfold as John had told me beforehand it would take that amount for me to get back to Tel Aviv. In one service, I took $1 out of my reserved $10 to put in the collection plate, thinking I would ask John for $1 when I got ready to go to Tel Aviv. The next morning as I was walking and praying and on my way back to the flat, I stepped up on the sidewalk and there lay $1 of American money, exactly the amount I needed to complete the $10 for my ticket back to Tel Aviv. Knowing exactly where it came from and with a grateful heart, I picked it up.

Jane and I met a lady in one of our services who was visiting in Jerusalem and said she was moving from Capernaum to Jerusalem because of her love for the city. In talking, we mentioned that we wanted to see the Sea of Galilee and other Biblical sites. She told us she knew two ladies that had just opened up a place for rest and relaxation for a church out of Tulsa and said she would take us there to stay while she was packing to move. As it turned out, we learned after arriving we were their first guests and they let us stay free of charge. It was such a blessing as we were driven all around the Sea of Galilee where the water was so clear and calm, you could see the rocks and fish. I got up early one morning so I could see the sun rise over the Sea of Galilee and it was breathtaking, made even more amazing by the thought that Christ had walked there.

We were also taken to the mountain where Christ gave the Beatitudes and to Peter's house where Christ healed his mother-in-law. It was almost unbelievable to know I was gazing upon sites and walking in areas traveled by the disciples and followers of Christ. In Tiberius, we visited a place called the Valley of the Doves filled with large numbers of beautiful multicolored doves. From experiencing the sense of calmness which their presence brought, it was understandable why God chose them as a symbol of peace. Going from place to place, I realized how far Christ had walked in going from the Sea of Galilee to all these different places.

Driving back, we stopped at the Jordan River. There was somewhat of a contrast between it and the Sea of Galilee. The Jordan River was not as clear as the Sea of Galilee, but remembering it was the place where Jesus was baptized made it beautiful to behold. I doused my feet in it for just a few minutes so I could say I had been in the Jordan River.

One day as I was getting ready to go for my daily routine of walking and praying, I had a loose button on my blouse and realized I had forgotten my needles and thread, which I always carried with me. As I walked and prayed, I saw something shiny a few feet ahead of me and wondered what it was. As I walked up to it, I realized it was a brand new needle. Thankfully, the button had enough thread that I was able to sew it back on. Remembering the things God puts in my path when I am in need, I never hesitate to investigate any curious object in my path. It could be another blessing just waiting.

Passover began while I was there and a group of inter-cessors we had met from England was going to meet at the Upper Room to pray and they invited me to attend. They told me what gate to go through to get there and I told the cab driver. He took me to the Damascus Gate instead, which was a great distance below the Upper Room. Knowing the room was up, I started walking, trying to find my way. As always, I had my staff with me. After much walking, I stopped a lady and asked where the Upper Room was. She said, "I'm a Jew," indicating she did not acknowledge the Upper Room. I decided the next time, I would ask where David's Tomb was as I knew it was close to the Upper Room and felt sure I could find my way from there.

After getting directions to David's Tomb from another lady, I began walking again. It was very hot that day, and after walking a while longer without finding it, I noticed a lady waving her arms at me, saying, "Hurry...come... they're waiting for you." She continued, saying, "My husband is looking for you." A man then joined her and they took me to the Upper Room.

After getting there, I told them I was so thirsty and would love to have a bottle of water. The man handed me a large bottle of ice cold water. I turned to thank him and in the blink of an eye, they were gone. I am convinced they were angels sent by God to guide me as He knew I was lost. And He sent an added blessing of water with them. During the Upper Room service, all I could do was cry, recognizing God's presence with me in that place.

David's tomb was located below the Upper Room and was quite impressive, although in visiting the site, the Holy Spirit's presence did not overwhelm me as in the Upper Room. Still, it was quite a feeling to know I was looking at the tomb where King David is thought to be buried.

The next week, a large group of people from South Africa was coming and John asked me to let them use my room. Since we were not going to have anywhere to stay, John arranged for Jane and me to stay with an American lady who had rented a large place in the Arab region. While staying in that region, I walked the historical road of

Jericho and remembered how the Israelites, in spite of the impenetrable walls of Jericho, had miraculously conquered the city, relying on the protection of almighty God.

At church, I met a man from Australia who had lived in Israel for some time. He told us he had burned his passport so they could not make him leave. They would put him in jail once in a while for a few days and would then release him. He had such a love for Israel, he was willing to spend these times in jail if it meant he did not have to leave. We were thrilled when he asked Jane and me if we would like to go on a tour. Naturally, we did. Among other places, he took us to where Jesus rode the donkey into Jerusalem and to the Pool of Siloam, told about in John 9 as the place where Jesus healed the blind man. We saw the palace where David lived and where he gazed upon Bathsheba for the first time. It was such a wonderful feeling to see the places told about in the Bible and be able to see them for ourselves.

After walking these long distances, I noticed I was not even tired. On this and previous trips, although staying sometimes for two months in one country, I never once became ill or even experienced a headache. God kept me healthy at all times so that I could minister and accomplish His tasks.

Jane knew some people preparing to go to Jordan and we asked if we could go. I had a desire to see the Dead Sea but didn't know if I would get the opportunity. I was so happy when the bus stopped for a fifteen minute rest period at the Dead Sea. There were many people swimming, or I should say floating in the water, but Jane and I chose to only put our hands in. We had not brought our bathing suits along, but due to our time schedule, we did not have the time anyway.

When we entered Jordan, we were told not to say "hallelujah," "praise the Lord," or anything pertaining to Jehovah God. This was because the country of Jordan is not a Christian nation. When we crossed into Jordan, Jane and I observed a very large body of water. Thinking it was the Red Sea, we went down and put the staff into the water, hoping God might have a miracle in mind for us. Nothing unusual happened but we weren't discouraged. We always took advantage of any given opportunity to witness and experience whatever He *did* have in store.

While in Jordan, Jane and I lived in a church apartment which had been provided for the seamen to come and rest. While there, we met two young girls: one from New York and one from Florida. They said God had told them to go to Saudi Arabia; although they did not understand why, they were going in obedience to God. On a Friday evening, we met for a Seder dinner with the two American girls, the people with whom we had gone to Jordan, and a professor from Australia and his wife. The Seder dinner is part of the Jewish ritual feast marking the beginning of Passover.

After praying for a while, one of the girls walked up to me and said, "You have a Word from God." Immediately, I spoke the words, "Take the staff and climb the mountain where Aaron is buried." Voicing that I had no idea where this location was, the gentleman from Australia said it was Mount Hor. He said he knew where it was and had always wanted to climb it. Everyone enthusiastically began to make plans for me to go there with him and his wife. As usual, I was low on funds and the professor and his wife offered to pay for the trip. A guide from Petra was hired and upon arriving at our destination, he asked if we wanted to ride a camel or a donkey. We chose the donkey as they can climb farther and higher than camels. We rode them as far as they could climb and then walked and climbed the rest of the way.

When we stopped for lunch at the top of the mountain, there was a couple already there eating lunch and we sat down and joined them. In visiting with them, we learned it was their job to maintain Aaron's tomb, and after discovering our reason for being there, they offered to take us to the place where Aaron was *supposedly* buried. It was a large tomb covered with just a cloth. After we looked at it, the lady then told us if we had a flashlight, she would take us into the mountain where Aaron was *actually* buried.

Fortunately, the gentleman from Australia had a flashlight so she led us down inside the mountain and assured us again this was Aaron's actual burial place. It was a wall with a recessed place into the mountain with only a cloth covering it. No one coming there was ever allowed to touch it. As we started out, we were recounting how the Bible says in one instance that "three went up into the mountain and two came down." We jokingly wondered if we three went up, would only two come down, and which two would that be? It was amusing to discuss the possibility.

Coming up from the mountain cave, I stood up and raised the staff over my head. All I heard the Father say was "Come...come from the North and the South... come from the East and the West." He was inviting His people to come to Him as the Jews return to their home place, Israel.

Petra was another beautiful place. It was covered with rose rock. I can't put into words my feelings when I remembered how the Israelites fought there and how God protected them and gave them victory in the battle.

After leaving Petra, Jane and I returned to Jerusalem. At the next meeting we attended, the pastor asked me to tell about my trip and the Rod of Grace. He had spoken that evening about the grace of God and thought my telling it would further emphasize that grace. He asked me to bring the staff forward, and when I did, he put one end on my shoulder and the other on his. He placed a prayer shawl over the rod and said if anyone there would like more of God's grace to come pass under the rod. Each person came under the power of God as they passed under the rod and fell to the floor. When the last person had passed under the rod, the pastor and I were the only ones left standing with a room full of those who had fallen.

I left Israel with mixed feelings. I had met so many different people there and shared so many wonderful experiences. I had been invited by different ladies into their home to share what they referred to as "salad lunches." The fellowship was always warm and welcoming and the food was delicious. The opportunity of seeing their homes and how they lived just increased my desire to make Israel my home. I still have that desire today.

My travels to so many countries has left me in wonder at all the many creations of every kind, human and animal, which God has made. It makes one realize how great, wonderful and powerful our almighty Father is when we see his beautiful workmanship, knowing He is everywhere in everything we see. In every nation I walk, He is always with me, leading and providing my every need in all situations.

How can I thank Him for the wisdom, power and love He bestows upon me? He is still with me today in the small town of Newcastle, Oklahoma, as I pray for this land as I have for so many lands before, seeing souls that need salvation as the natives of Africa, India, Ghana and all lands do. I pray that God will pour out his spirit upon all flesh in these last days, as foretold in Acts 2:17. That souls will be saved and our spirits will be freed to praise and worship the Lord in complete surrender to His will.

My sole purpose in telling my story is to instill in each reader that my amazing walk and close fellowship with the Holy Spirit is available to any believer who desires more and more of God. There is and was nothing in my life that set me apart from anyone else, except perhaps my overwhelming love for Him and a burning desire which He placed within my spirit to experience all God had for me.

So many Christians today do not realize what Christ meant when he said "I have come that they might have life, and that they might have it more abundantly."

Abundantly means "to the fullest." How many of us are living our daily lives as Christians to the fullest? God longs for a close daily relationship and communion with each of us, just as He did with Adam and Eve from the beginning in the Garden. What that proclamation means to me, and should mean to every child of God, is that Christ, by giving His life for us, and by being our substitute for the sins we have committed or will ever commit, did not suffer death so that we might just rest in the assurance of our salvation and seek nothing else.

Yes, it is wonderful to think of our eternal home and of the wonder of being in the presence of the one and only almighty God throughout eternity, but His suffering and death means so much more. He wants us to experience and enjoy that same holy presence in our lives each day, and to talk to Him as we would with a dear friend or loving parent. To go to Him in prayer with our gratitude and praise and to lay our hearts bare at his throne of mercy. To lay before Him our needs, our burdens, and our cries for healing in body and spirit to the one of whom it is said "By His stripes, we are healed."

Have you ever wondered what it would be like to actually hear the voice of God? Is there any scripture in His Word that says He quit speaking to His children after Noah or Moses or Paul? God is as much alive today and as willing to speak to us as He was then if we are willing to listen. Our lack of faith to believe He will actually speak to us is the only thing keeping us from hearing Him. Pray for that kind of faith. Seek His will for your life. Go to Him in prayer with a willing heart and spirit, anticipating you *will* hear Him, and after hearing, you will obey.

It's not always easy. Sometimes sacrifices are required. When He told me to quit my job and sell everything I had, I didn't immediately jump for joy at the thought of being homeless and without income. But I had no doubt as to what God had told me to do, and in knowing this, stepped out on faith and obeyed. God has never failed in providing for me. Even when situations looked like there was no hope, His love shined through with need after need being met.

Throughout all my travels, sometimes anxious situations, and yes, sometimes fear of the unknown awaiting me, my comfort and my constant companion was, and remains, the overwhelming and amazing love and presence of the Holy Spirit. My journey truly was a walk of faith in a heart willing to be led by the Holy Spirit and sustained daily by the grace of God. As He has said, "Behold, I am with you always, even to the end of the age."

A couple of years ago, I was reading my Bible and I looked up and saw the face of Jesus saying, "Tell them I'm coming…I'm coming." Through the telling of my story, I have tried earnestly to impart to others the unspeakable joy that comes from a close, personal relationship with the Holy Spirit. My prayer is that every believer reading this book will long for and receive that joy.

> "EYE HATH NOT SEEN, NOR EAR HEARD, NEITHER HAVE ENTERED INTO THE HEART OF MAN, THE THINGS WHICH GOD HATH PREPARED FOR THEM THAT LOVE HIM." (1st CORINTHIANS 2:9)

Coming upon my 92nd birthday in a few months, I can do nothing but rejoice at the anticipation of going home to my blessed Savior. To look at last into the righteous face of the one who suffered, bled and died for me. To have his precious nail-scarred hand take mine, and to have Him say unto me, "Well done, good and faithful servant…enter now into the joy of the Lord."

Hallelujah!
And the Spirit and the bride say "Come."

60482858R00069

Made in the USA
Lexington, KY
08 February 2017